The New
Geordie Dictionary

edited by Frank Graham

ISBN-13   978-0-946928-11-8
ISBN-10   0946928118
This reprint 2013

Originally published by Frank Graham
Published by Butler Publishing in 1987
©1987 Butler Publishing, Thropton, Morpeth, Northumberland, NE65 7LP

Butler
publishing

INTRODUCTION

This dictionary could probably be described as an abbreviation of Heslop's *Northumberland Words* (1892). It is based on that local book and most of the examples are taken from it. Only occasionally have we used inverted commas to show that we are quoting from Heslop, especially where the quotation is lengthy. Cecil Geeson's *Northumberland and Durham Word Book* (1969) is based on Heslop's work but contains a number of entries which have been useful to our dictionary. In 1974 we published a *Geordie Dictionary* in a limited edition. We have not yet reprinted this work since we felt it needed considerable revision and thought it better to compile a new book. Some of our entries may be similar to the *Geordie Dictionary* but this is because the book published in 1974 was also based almost entirely on Heslop and Geeson and probably 90% of it was direct quotations from these two books.

Heslop's work contains a large number of words which are now obsolete. In the present book we have in most cases only included words and phrases which are still current. For a simple and short dictionary of Geordie dialect today the reader will find Todd's *Geordie Words and Phrases* the best introduction.

There is no definitive Geordie dialect. There are considerable variations in the speech spoken in Northumberland and Durham, partly geographical changing from north to south, partly occupational as illustrated by the mining and farming communities. The urban areas, particularly Tyneside, have also developed words and phrases with different meanings from those used in the rural districts. So we are using the word *Geordie* in a very loose and general sense.

We have only occasionally referred to pronunciation. The subject is too complicated to be treated in this small book. Pronunciation, however, has infinite variations in our area. *Geordie* has always been a living dialect, changing and developing, therefore many words have changed over the centuries. Sometimes we have noted these changes. However to understand and appreciate our dialect you must hear it spoken. For this purpose our dictionary is unfortunately of little use.

WHO IS A GEORDIE?

The origin of the word *Geordie* has been a matter of much discussion and controversy. All the explanations are fanciful and not a single piece of genuine evidence has ever been produced. For many years I have been trying to ascertain the first time the word was used, hoping thereby to find some clue as to its origin. The first record of its use that I have found was in 1823. The speaker was the famous local comedian, Billy Purvis, who had set up his booth at the Newcastle Races on the Town Moor. He had, however, a competitor. A well known showman had erected his tent nearby and had employed a young pitman called Tom Johnson to act the part of the clown. This incensed Billy Purvis who engaged in a personal tirade against his rival. Hearing that he had sold his furniture and left his wife to become a clown Billy cried out:

Ah. man, wee but a feul wad hae sold off his furnitor and left his wife. Noo, yor a fair doon reet feul, not an artificial feul like Billy Purvis! Thous a real Geordie! gan man an hide thysel! gan an' get thy picks agyen. Thou may de for the city, but never for the west end o' wor toon.

From this account we can see clearly that in 1823 *Geordie* was a fool. The explanation is obvious. In 1788 George III who was a very unpopular monarch became insane and although he recovered for a while his son (later George IV) had to be made Regent in 1811 and continued to perform that office until the insane monarch died. George IV was also unpopular. His extravagance, his love of pleasure and his promiscuity were notorious. When he became king in January 1820 he started proceedings to divorce his wife Caroline. All those who disliked the Hanoverian monarchy united to defend her. In 1820 there was a gigantic demonstration in Newcastle in support of the Queen.

We can understand therefore how the word *Geordie* was a term of abuse and was linked with idiocy. In the 19th century (and much later) the middle class of Newcastle disliked and feared the mining community and they probably used the word *Geordie* as a term of abuse when they referred to pitmen, and the word became linked to them. In England many people try to forget any disagreeable characteristics of their monarchs as quickly as possible. When the early Hanoverians passed away *Geordie* gradually ceased to be an insulting word and eventually was accepted as a friendly term when applied not only to pitmen but anyone who lived in this area.

So in a little over fifty years a term of abuse became an accepted name when the insane George III, from whom the word was derived, had been forgotten.

A

A. A preposition – on. *A this side* – on this side.

A. A verb. *Aa wad a thowt se* – I would have thought so.

AA. Pronoun of the first person. *Aa divvin' knaa* – I do not know. In local works it is usually spelt *aw*.

AA. All. *Thor aa' gyen* – They are all gone. *It's aa ower* – It's all over.

AA. To owe. *Aa aa nowt* – I owe nothing.

ABACKA BEYONT. Far away. *He lives abacka beyont.*

AABUT. Almost – *allbut*.

AAD. Old. *An aad wife* – an old woman. *Canny aad soul* – nice old soul. *Owld* is another form of the word.

AA'D. I had. *Aa'd better gan canny* – I had better be careful.

AA'D. I would. *Aa'd a been there mesel* – I would have been there myself.

AAD-FASHINT. Old fashioned.

AAFUL. Awful. She set off the *aafulest* shrieks.

AAKWAAD. Awkward.

AAL. All. *Aal reet* – all right. *Aall togither like the folks o' Shields* – This Tyneside proverb illustrates the clannishness of the people of Shields.

AAN. Own. *Me aan fireside.*

AA WARND. I suppose. *Aa-warnd ye think yorsel' clivvor?*. I suppose you think yourself clever.

ABLEEZE. On fire.

ADIT. Horizontal gallery for draining a mine.

AE. One.
"Tweed says to Till,
What gars ye rin sae ill?
Sae still as I rin, and sae fast as ye gae,
Where ye drawn *ae* man, I drawn twae."

AFEARD. Afraid. *Thor's nowt to be afeared on*. There's nothing to be afraid of.

AGYEN. Again.

AHAD. Hold. *Get ahad on't*. Get a hold on it.

AHINT. Behind. "There was a man following *ahint* to pick up the fish that were killed". S. Oliver's *Rambles in Northumberland, 1835. Come in ahint* was the drover's cry to his dog.

ALLER. The alder.

AMANG. Among.

AMAIN. Without check. When a set of waggons breaks loose they are said to *run amain.*

ARGIE. To argue. *Divvent argie.* Don't argue. Also the phrase *argyin' the toss.*

ARSE. Backside. An *arse-loop* was a wide loop in the rope by which a man was supported when repairing a pit-shaft.

ASSAY. I say. *Assay, what are ye dein there?*

ATWIX. Between.

AX. Ask. *Ax wor lass.* Ask my wife.

AYE. Yes. A word continually used – *why aye* – Of course.

AYONT. Behind. See Hexham proverb "He comes from Hexham Green, and that's ten miles *ayont* Hell."

B

BAAD. Ill.

BAAL. A ball. *A stottin-baal* – a bouncing ball. *A clooty ball* – a ball made of rags.

BACK END. A term for autumn.

BACK-SHIFT. There are two shifts normally worked down the pit. The first is the fore-shift, the second is the back-shift.

BACK-SIDE. The back of a building. Billy Purvis used to ask the crowd from his front stage to enter his show, saying: "Them 'at dissent like to waak ower the stage can come in bi Billy's *backside.*

BACKSIDE. Buttocks, arse or *hint end.*

BAD. Ill. *He lucks, poor body, verra bad. He's had one of his bad torns.*

BADLY-LIKED. Disliked.

BADLY-OFF. Poor.

BAD-MAN'S OATMEAL. The flower and seed of the hemlock.

BAD-WEATHER GEORDY. A name applied to cockle sellers. "As the season at which cockles are in greatest demand is generally the most stormy in the year – September to March – the sailors' wives at the seaport towns of Northumberland and Durham consider the cry of the cockle man as the harbinger of bad weather, and the sailor, when he hears the cry of 'cockles alive,' in a dark wintry night, concludes that a storm is at hand, and breathes a prayer, backwards, for the soul of *Bad-Weather-Geordy.'* – S. Oliver, *Rambles in Northumberland,* 1835.

BAFF. This word means a "blank". When pitmen were paid fortnightly one week was pay week and the other was the *baff* week.

>"The *Baff* week is o'er – no repining –
>Pay Saturday's swift on the wing".

BAGIE. The belly. Also applies to the turnip.

BAIRN. A child. A homely word which denotes affection. *A bit bairn. Geordie haed the bairn* – Geordie haed the bairn. A well known song.

BAIST. To beat.

BAIT. Food. BAIT-POKE or BAIT-CAN. A metal container to carry food to work.

BANG. To strike violently or to excel. *The blacksmith's hammer yark for yark, we hear no longer bangin'.*
Up the raa. Thou bangs thee muthor me canny bairn. You are better than your mother. Local song.

BANK. A steep road or incline. Not a hill as often suggested. See Byker Bank, Newcastle, Battle Bank, Gateshead.

BANKED UP. Applied to coal piled up at the colliery or on the fire.

BANKSMAN. The man in control at the top of the shaft of a pit.

BANKY. With many banks or gradients. *A banky road.*

BANNOCK. A thick cake of oat, barley or peas meal usually unleavened. Gaelic in origin.

BANTY. A bantam.

BAP. A baker's roll. *A penny bap.*

BARGIE. A claim.

BARK. A bad cough. *He was barkin' his heed off.*

BARLEY. To claim. Almost always used by children in games. *Aa barleyed forst kick.*

BARNEY. A fight or argument.

BARRAS. Obsolete word for a barrier in front of a fortress. Here tournaments were held. BARRAS BRIDGE at Newcastle derives its name from the knightly encounters which took place there.

BARRY. To bury.

BASH. To hit with violence. *She bashed the door i' me fyece.* She closed the door in my face.

BASIN CROP. Hair of head cut straight round a basin.
Three apprentices, "showing themselves disobedient and very obstinate, were first in open court (where a dish is said to have been kept, by the edge of which their hair was cut round) made exemplary by shortninge their hair." – *Books of Merchant Adventurers,* Newcastle, December 7, 1649.

BASTE. To thrash. *Aa'll gie ye sic a byestin' as ye nivver got i' yor life. A baster* ball was one made of paper. It was attached to string and could be used to attack other children.

BAT. A blow. *A bat i' the feyce.* A blow in the face.

BATTER. A drinking bout. *He's on the batter agyen.* In recent years it refers to prostitution. *She's on the batter.*

BAY. An enclosure in outdoor children's games. Usually a place of safety. *Thoo canna catch me, noo aa's in the bay.*

BEAK. The nose.

BECK. A small stream, The name occurs sixty-three times in Durham but not in Northumberland (Wansbeck is not an exception.

BED-GOON. A bed gown and also a loose jacket worn by women in the harvest field. Later applied to any loose working garment worn by women. *Hor bedgoon is laelock.* – Her jacket is lilac in colour. (Cushie Butterfield).

BEGOX. By God.

BEHINT. Behind (but ahint is commoner).

BELAA. Below.

BELLYFLAPPER. A blow on the stomach by landing flat when diving into the water.

BELLY-TIMMER. Food.

> *This was the kind o' belly-timmer,*
> *For myeken pitmen strang and tuiff.*
> Pitman's Pay.

BET. Bruised by heavy walking. *A bet foot.*

BEUK. A book.

BEYUT. To boot. Something additional paid in a case of barter. For instance in bartering horses one will say "I will give you a pound *te beyut*" i.e. a pound extra.

BID. To invite or command. Usually applied to a funeral or wedding so that a refusal was considered an insult. *Dee as yer bid* – Do what your told. Those who went round with the invitations were called *bidders.*

BIDE. Wait. *Bide heor.* Wait here. Abide. *Aa canna bide yon chap.* Stay. *Bide a bit.*

BIGG. Barley. Barley was once sold in Newcastle *Bigg Market.*

BIGGIN. A building. Hence the place called *Newbiggen.* Also used in pits for a built up pillar of stones.

BILE. A boil. *Me bile's borst.*

BILLY. A companion. *Ye silly billy* is a friendly term.

BIN. *Hoo bin ye the day.* How are you today.

BINDIN. A term used when keelmen or pitmen contracted to work for a long period, usually a year.

BING. A measure for lead. 8 cwts.

BIRKIE. A smart fellow. Usually not an offensive term

BITCH. To spoil some work. *Ye've myed a bitch on't.* You have spoilt it.

BLAA. Breath. *Get yor blaa.* Rest till your breath comes back.

BLAA. To blow. *Blaa the leet oot.* Blow out the light.

BLAA OOT. A "blow out", a drinking bout.

BLABB. To talk loosley. *He'll blabber and taak all neet.* Hence the term *blabber.*

BLACK-DAM. Carbonic acid gas sometimes encountered in pits.

BLACK DIAMONDS. Coal.

BLACKEY. The blackbird.

BLACK PUDDEN. A food made of blood, suet, and herbs stuffed into the intestines of a pig or sheep. Brockett (1846) tells us, "This savoury and piquant delicacy is a standing dish among the people of the North."

BLAIR. *The bairns were blairin'.*

BLASH. Any weak drink. Clarty *Blash tea* – weak tea. *Their streets are like wors – brave and blashy.* T. Thompson, *Canny Newcastle.*

BLATHER. To talk nonsense. *He jawed a heap of blather.* He talked a load of nonsense.

BLATHER SKITE. One who talks aimlessly.

BLEB. A blister.

BLEEZER. A metal sheet, to blow up a fire by increasing the draught.

BLOGGED. Blocked. Refers to spouts and pipes.

BLOOD ALLEY. A boy's marble, with blue or red lines.

BODY. A person. *She's a canny aad body.*

BOGIE. A small, low, four-wheeled cart. Often used by children for play. "In Dean Street, when carts or bogies came down, the noise made one's heart glad, one's lugs fit to strain," **Gilchrist, 1835.**

BOILEY. Milk and bread boiled.

BONDAGER. A Northumbrian word to describe a female field-worker whom the "hind" had to supply when he contracted to work for a farmer.

BONE. To interrogate.

BONNY. Good looking. But is usually used like "canny" to describe character as well as looks. A *bonny bairn,* a good looking child. *A bonny singer,* an accomplished singer. Sometimes it is used ironically to describe the opposite, *a bonny mess; thor's a bonny game gaan en.* The old song says:-
"My *bonny* keel laddie. my *canny* keel laddie,"

BOODY. A piece of broken pot. *Bits o' boodies.*

BOOL. Bowl. To play at boolin, a game popular in the north also means to bowl along as in *bool your hoop.*

BOOZE. Drink. *He's on the booze* – he's on a drinking bout.

BORD. A bird. Today slang for a girl.

BORN. In Northumberland means a burn or large stream. See Ouseburn, Newcastle.

BORST. Burst.

BOWK. To belch.

BOWLD. Bold.

BRAN NEW. Brand new, quite new.

BRANKS. A bridle to gag nagging women especially used in Newcastle. "Tbe branks, a kind of brake is here, Wor faithers when a' else was vain, compelled the noisy jades to weer. Where'er their clappers rain amain." Thomas Wilson.

BRASS. Money.

BRAT. A disagreeable child.

BRAY. To beat.

BRAZEN. Impudent, shameless. *She's a brazen hussey.*

BREED. Bread.

BREEKS. Trousers. *A bran new coat, but aad breeks.* A new coat but old trousers.

BREWSTER. Brewer. Hence the Brewster Sessions where publicans apply for their licenses.

BROCK. Badger.

BROON. Brown.

BUBBLE. To weep. *Give ower bubblin'* – Stop crying.

BUBBLY JOCK. Turkey cock. Probably so called from the wattles hanging down his neck.

BUFF. The bare skin. *Stripped to the buff.*

BUGGER. A rough term of affection in the North. *A canny aad bugger.*

BULLETS. Sweets. So called from the shape of a bullet. The best known were *black bullets,* still manufactured. *Sells bullets and claggum for bairns.* Wilson's Songs, 1890.

BULLY. A brother, comrade. The crew of a keel were called *bullies.*

BUM. Buttocks.

BUMMLER BOX. A small house.

BUMMLER. A bee.

BUMS. Bailiffs who distrain. Some times called a *bum bailiff* from the practice of touching the debtor on the back.

BUSS. A kiss.

BUT AND BEN. Outside and inside. Refers to two-roomed houses with an outer and inner room.

BUZZEMS. Besoms or brooms made of twigs. The song *Buy Broom Buzzems* was made famous by William Purvis (Blind Willie) born in Newcastle about 1752.

BYEUT. Boot. *A byeut i' the hintend.* A kick in the backside.

C

CAA. Call. *Caa oot* – Call out. Also 'to drive'. See the song – *Caa Hawkie through the watter.*

CAAD. Cold.

CADGE. To beg.

CADGER. Originally one who went from house to house buying and selling butter, eggs, corn and other farm produce. Nowadays the term is only used for a beggar.

CAIRN. Pile of stones over a grave or on a mountain top.

CAKHOUSE. A latrine.

CAKKY. Animal or human waste.

CALLER. Fresh. *Caller herrin* – a well known street cry.

CANDYMAN. A bum bailiff. The man who serves notice of ejectment. The word is almost always used as a term of abuse or contempt. The reason for this is the way these men were regularly used during mining strikes. Pitmen lived in "tied" houses and if they went on strike the coal owners usually evicted them. To do so many bailiffs were needed. They were recruited from the scum of the towns and many street vendors were among those so employed. Some of the street traders sold sticks of candy, their street cry being *Dandy-candy, three sticks a penny*. So all bum bailiffs were contemptuously described as *candymen*.

CANNY. The most common and most beautiful word in our dialect. We cannot better Heslop's description:

"An embodiment of all that is kindly, good, and gentle. The highest compliment that can be paid to any person is to say that he or she is *canny*. As "home" expresses the English love of the fireside, so in Tyneside and Northumberland does *canny* express every home virtue. All that is good and loveable in man or woman is covered by the expression "Eh, what a *canny* body !" A child appealing for help or protection always addresses his elder as *canny* man "Please. *canny* man, gi's a lift i' yor cairt." "O, *canny* man O show me the way to Wallington." What Northumberland bairn but has appealed, when punishment impended, "Please *canny* man, it wasn't me !" The fishwife who wishes to compliment her customer says, "Noo, *canny*-hinny, see what yor buyin'."

CANNY TOON. Newcastle has long been known to its inhabitants by this description. The first written record is Oliver's *Songs, 1824. Sic wonders there happens in wor canny toon.*

CANT. An angle greater than a right angle. A tip-over.

CANTY. Pleasant, lively. *My canny keel laddie, so hansum se canty, and free, O ! The Sandgate Lassie,* H. Robson.

CAP. To surpass.

CAPPY. A boy's game. Also the name of the dog in the famous song of that name.

CARLINGS. A Northumbrian correspondent to the *Gentleman's* Magazine, 1788 writes:

"choice grey-peas, of the preceding autumn steeped in spring water for twelve or fifteen hours, till they are soaked or macerated; then laid on a sieve, in the open air, that they may be externally dry. Thus swelled, and enlarged to ·a considerable size, and on the verge of vegetating, they are put in an iron pot, or otherwise, on a slow fire, and kept stirring. They will then parch, crack, and as we provincially call it, bristle: when they begin to burn, they are ready to eat."

Carling Sunday is the second Sunday before Easter and traditionally they are served on that day. It is almost certainly connected with religion. The story that the custom started when a famine in Newcastle was relieved by the arrival of a ship loaded with a cargo of grey peas has no foundation whatsoever.

CAUSEY. A causeway.

CAVIL. A distribution by lot. A word used by pitmen to describe the system whereby they drew lots to decide their work places in the pit. *I've gotten a canny cavil for this quarter.*

CHAAK. Chalk.

CHAMPION. First class.

CHARE. A narrow lane. A word once in common use in Newcastle. In 1800 there were 21 chares on the Quayside. They are found in several towns and villages of the north east. Hexham – *St. Mary's Chare.* Morpeth – *Copper Chare.* Holy Island – *Tripping Chare.*

> "A laughable misunderstanding happened at our assizes some years ago, when one of the witnesses in a criminal trial swore that *'he saw three men come out of the foot of a chare!'* 'Gentlemen of the jury,' exclaimed the learned judge, 'you must pay no regard to that man's evidence, he must be insane.' But the foreman, smiling, assured the judge that they understood him very well, and that he spoke the words of truth and soberness."
> *(An Impartial History of Newcastle, 1801).*

CHECK-WEIGHMAN. A representative of the colliers who checks the weight of coal at the surface on behalf of his men.

CHEOR. A popular salutation – *What cheor ?*

CHEESE. To set the cheese on the table upside down was once considered a mark of disrespect. There is a famous Border tongue twister:

> "The folk of Chatton say the cheese of Chatton is better than the cheese of Chillingham; but the cheese of Chatton's nee mair like the cheese of Chillingham than chalk's like cheese."

CHEP. Chap. *Canny aad chep.*

CHESTER. A Roman camp. There are twenty six place names in Northumberland combined with this word. Elsewhere the word is usually *caster* or *cester.*

CHIEL. A friend. More a Border than a Geordie term.

CHIMLEY. Chimney. *Chimley-neuk* – chimney corner.

CHINE. Chain. The Scotswood suspension bridge was called the *Chine Bridge.*

CHINK. Money.

CHITTER-CHATTER. Idle prattle.

CHIVES. Wild onion found on the Roman Wall.

CHOKE-DAMP. Also called *after-damp,* the result of an explosion of fire-damp down the mine.

CHOLLER. A double chin.

CHORCH. Church.

CHOW. To chew.

CHOWK. To choke. *Bring me a drink – aa's fit te chowk.*

CHUCK. Bread.

CHUCKS. A game played by children with pebbles called *chuckie stones.*

CHUNTER. To grumble. *She's alwes chunteren on, nivvor content wi nowt* – a local saying.

CLAA. A claw.

CLAES. Clothes. A *claes-prop* was used to hold up the washing line.

CLAG. To stick.

CLAGGUM. Toffee made with treacle.

CLAGGY. Sticky. *claggy taffy* – sticky toffee.

CLAMMING. Hungry, thirsty. Usually used in the expression: *I'm clamming for a drink.*

CLARTS. Mud. *"Wi' clarts they should be plastered well, that jeer'd Blind Willie's singing."* "He's just clartin on" means he is messing about. *Common as clarts* is a derogatory expression.

CLASH. To strike or close violently. *Divvin' clash the door* – Do not slam the door. Then we have a witness's statement at a trial in Newcastle. *He clashed his jaa; an then clagged up his eye wi' clarts.*

CLATTER. A noise.

CLEG. Gadfly.

CLEUGH. Pronounced *cluff.* Well explained by S. Oliver in *Rambles in Northumberland,* 1835. "A *hope* is the head of a vale, a *cleugh* is a sort of diminitive *hope,* where the vale is narrowed by opposite *craigs.*

CLICK. To snatch. *He clicked it oot o' me hand.* Also means a tear – *a greet click iv her frock.*

CLIP. To strike. *Aa'll clip your lug* – I will strike your ear.

CLIVVOR. Clever. Also in good health. *How are ye the day, lad? Man, aa's clivvor.*

CLOBBER. Clothes.

CLOCKER. A sitting hen. *What are ye sittin clockin theor at?* – Why are you sitting for such a long time?

CLOD. A penny in the Tyneside dialect.

CLOG. A shoe with a wooden sole. Once very common on Tyneside. There were several clog shops in Castle Garth Stairs before the war.

CLOOTIE BAAL. A ball made with rags and used by children as a football.

CLOSE. A small enclosure or narrow street as the *Close* at Newcastle.

CLOT. A stupid fellow.

CLOUT. To strike. *Aa'll cloot yor jaw.* A cloth. *dish-clout, clooty-mat* etc.

COB. Loaf of bread.

COBLE. The north-east fishing boat. It was deckless, flat bottomed and square at the stern.

COCKED. Drunk.

COCK-EYED. Squint-eyed.

COCKLE. Spit.

COCKTAIL. Warm ale with ginger. *At ivery yell hoose i' this toon we had a cocktail pot.* J. P. Robson.

COD. To lie, to pretend. *Whe are ye coddin?*

CODGER. See Cadger.

COGGLY. Unsteady. *The plank wis se coggly at aa nearly tummeled off.*

COIN. Turn. *Coin oot o' the way* – turn aside.

COLLEY. A lamplighter. The trade and name now obsolete. The Newcastle street song says: *Colley wiv a lamp, Colley wiv a leet, Colley wiv a little dog barkin at his feet.*

COLLIER. A pitman. One of the oldest terms in the coal trade but for a century rarely used locally. Also means a sea-going vessel carrying coals.

COME AND GAN. A Tyneside expression which means a good store of things. *Thor's plenty to come an gan on.*

COME BYE. Get out of the way.

COME THEE WAYS. Come forward. A friendly expression.

COMIN-ON. It's raining.

CONK. The nose.

CONKERS. Horse chestnuts. Also the name of the game played with them.

CONSART. Concert.

COO. Cow. Also an immoral woman.

COPPLE. To turn over. *Copple your creels* – a somersault.

CORF. Basket once used for taking coal from pits.

CORKER. A smart reply.

CORPORATION. The stomach.

COTTERILS. Money.

COWP. To upset. Mostly found in the expression *Cowp yor creels,* meaning to turn a somersault.

COWT. A colt. Also a man of strength. *Cowtale* was the allowance given to a blacksmith when a horse is first shod.

CRAA. A rook. *As black as a craa* – dirty.

CRABBY. Bad-tempered. *He's a crabby aad chep.*

CRACK. Gossip. *To hev a bit crack.*

CRACKER. A half-wit. Also firework.

CRACKET. A low stool.

CRANKY. An old term for pitmen. The word was probably derived from the checked pattern favoured by colliers. *A cranky neckcloth.*

> "'A pat on my blue coat that shines se,
> My jacket wi' posies se fine see,
>   My sark sic sma' threed, man,
>   My pig-tail se greet, man,
> Od smash ! what a buck was Bob *Cranky*.
>
> Blue stockings, white clocks, and reed garters,
> Yellow breeks, and my shoon wi' lang quarters,
>   A' myed wour bairns cry,
>   Eh ! sarties ! ni ! ni !
> When they saw the smart, clever Bob *Cranky*."
> *Bob Cranky's Size Sunday,* 1804.

Howky was another name used for a pitman. But early in the 19th century both terms were replaced by the word *Geordie*.

CREE. A small hut or pen. *Chicken cree.*

CREEL. A basket of wickerwork carried on the back and used to carry hay to sheep in bad weather. The *creel* of a Cullercoats fish-wife is well known.

CREEPS. Dislike or horror. *It gives me the creeps.*

CROAK. To give up the ghost.

CROFT. A small enclosure.

CROOD. Crowd. *The hoose is crooded out.*

CROON. Crown.

CROP. To cut the hair. *What a crop he's gien ye !*

CROWDY. Oatmeal and boiling water stirred together. An old Northumbrian dish. It is served with butter, dripping or milk – *The crowdy is wor daily dish.* T. Wilson. Pitman's Pay.

CROWLEY'S CREW. These were the men employed at the historic ironworks of Crowley and Co. at Swalwell and Winlaton. They were proud craftsmen. They could make anything *frev a needle tiv an anchor*. They were also political radicals.

CUDDLE. An embrace. "So then with a kiss and a cuddle these lovers they bent their way hyem." *The Pitman's Courtship.*

CUDDY. A donkey or a small horse. Also common abbreviation of Cuthbert.

CUDDY'S LEGS. An expression peculiar to the Newcastle Fish Market. It means herrings.

CULL. A stupid fellow.

CUNDY. A sewer.

CUSHAT. Old name for the ringdove.

CUT. Excavation through a hill.

CUTHBERT'S BEADS. Bits of fosil encrinites common on the beaches of Holy Island. Hence the name after St. Cuthbert.

CUTTY. Short. Cutty-gun is slang for a short pipe.

CUTTY SARK. A short shirt. More commonly used across the Border than in Northumberland. Also the name of a famous ship.

CYEK. Cake.

CYUK. Cook. *She canna cyuk.*

D

DAB. Skilful. *He's a dab-hand at it.*

DAD. A blow. The origin of this word is unknown. In Northumberland the word is now obsolete. *He got sic a dad as he'll not forget.*

DAFT. Silly. A common word on Tyneside and in the rest of the country. *Thou'll drive me daft.*

DAFTY. A fool. *Ye'll hit somebody, ye dafty.*

DAGGER MONEY. A custom peculiar to Newcastle. This is a gold coin paid to the Assize Judges when they came from Carlisle. The road was considered so dangerous that the money was paid to provide an armed escort. The custom is still carried on.

DAMP. Gas.

DANG. To strike violently. *They dang wi' trees and burst the door.*

DARG. A day's work.

DARN CROOK. Origin rather obscure but probably means a crooked and dark street. Darn means "dark".

DASH. Drink made from a mixture of beer and lemonade.

DATAL MAN. A man employed by the day. Datalling means odd jobbing.

DE. Do. Before a vowel becomes *div. Div aa knaa him?* The negative is *divvint.*

DEAR KNAAS. An unusual expression which means "I do not know." *Dear knaas what aa's gan te dee?*

DEED. Died. *Deed an' gyen* - dead and gone. The Deed-hoose was the mortuary.

DEEF. Deaf.

DEIL. Devil. The word was often used in oaths as *Deel tyek ye!* The devil take you.

DEMEAN. To lower oneself. *A waddent demean mesel to de sic a thing.*

DENE. A valley through which a burn flows. There were once a a number of burns (now sewers) in Newcastle. Dean Street receives its name from the Lort burn.

DEPPITY. Deputy. The man in charge of a section of a mine. "The deputies go to work an hour before the hewers. Their work consists of supporting the roof with props of wood, removing props from old workings, changing air currents when necessary, and clearing away any sudden eruption of gas or fall of stone that might impede the work of the hewer." (Dr. R. Wilson, Coal Miners of Durham and Northumberland – Trans. of Tyneside Naturalists' Club, Vol. VI, p.203.)

DICKY BIRD. A small bird, always used as a term of endearment. When cameras were first used children were always told to watch for the "dicky bird".

DIKE. The word is used to mean both hedge and ditch. "When I was young and lusty I could loup a dyke." Song. *Sair Fail'd Hinny.*

DILLER. Used in the expression *A diller, a dollar, a ten o'clock scholar* – referred to an unwilling scholar.

DILLY. A small public carriage, but in Northumberland only used in reference to an old engine on the Wylam railway called *the Wylam dilly.*

DING. To strike. To knock violently.

DINNA, DINNET, DIVENT. Do not. All these words have the same meaning. They illustrate the richness of our dialect.

DIRTY. Wet weather. *A dirty night* – a rainy night.

DISN'T. Does not. *He disn't knaa nowt.*

DIVART. To amuse.

DODD, TOD. A fox. "This is the family name of one of the old 'grains' of North Tynedale, who have been located here from Saxon times. Reginald of Durham, writing about A.D. 1150 gives the history of their progenitor, one Eilaf, who with his companions bore the body of St. Cuthbert in the flight from Lindisfarne. Being changed into the shape of a fox his fellow monks prayed to God and St. Cuthbert to restore him to his human shape. And from that day all the race of Eilaf bore the name of Tod (Dodd), which, in the mother tongue, signifies a fox. – Dr. Charlton, *North Tynedale and its Four Surnames".* Heslop.

DOG-LOUP. A narrow strip of ground between two houses only wide enough for a dog to pass. See the Dog Loup Stairs near the Blackgate at Newcastle.

DOLLUP. A large piece.

DONSIE. Unlucky.

DOOK. A bathe. *Have ye had a dook yit.*

DOOK. To duck. *Dook yor heed* – Duck your head.

DOON-BYE. Down there. *Aa's gaan doon-bye* – I'm going down there.

DORSN'T. Dare not. *Folks dorsent say owt tiv him.*

DORTY. Dirty. *She's a dorty body.*

DOTHER. To shake. **DOTHERY.** Shaky.

DOTTLE. The tobacco left at the bottom of a pipe after smoking.

DOUR. Sour-looking. *He's a dour lookin' chep.*

DOWIE. Depressed. *Cheer up, hinny, dinna look dowie.*

DOWTOR. Daughter.

DOZZLE. Same as *dottle*.

DRAAS. Drawers. *A kist o' draas* – a chest of drawers.

DRAP. A drop.

DREED. To dread. *Aa's dreedin the worst hinny.*

DRIFT. A place driven to reach coal.

DROOND. To drown. *He droonded he' sell.*

DROONED-OOT. Refers to a colliery that has been flooded.

DROOTHY. Thirsty.

DRY-DIKE. A stone wall built without lime.

DUCCOT. Also called *pigeon-duccot or pigeon cree*. A dovecot.

DUCKS AND DRAKES. A children's game in which flat stones are thrown on water which tip the surface several times before sinking.

DUDS. Working clothes.

DUFF. Coal dust.

DUMP. Cigarette butt or *fag end*.

DUMPLIN. Pudding of dumplin and suet.

DUN. Yellowish brown colour. *A dun horse, a dun coo.*

DUNCH. To knock against. *Somebody dunched his airm.*

DUNT. To strike on the backside. Once a custom among school-boys who held the victim by the legs and arms and struck his behind against a stone. See Dunting Stone at Newbiggin. *(Curiosities of Northumberland).*

DUT. Bowler hat.

E

EE. Eye. *Come to me, ma little lammy, come, thou apple o' ma ee.*

EE. An expression of delight.

EE. You. *It was ee at did it* – It was you who did it.

ELWIS. Always.

ETTLE. To intend. *Aa'll ettle to be there, noo, if I can* – I intend to be there now, if I can.

EVERYS. A children's game of searching and when something is found everyone shouts *Everys*. The article found is then shared out.

F

FAAL. To fall.

FAALLEN WRANG. Become pregnant.

FACE. Mining term for the end of the working where the hewers work.

FAD. A hobby or whimsical fancy.

FADGE. A small flat loaf of bread generally made up from the dough left over from a baking.

FADGE. To eat together.

At Warkworth, "at the season of the New Year there is provided a rich cake with its usual accompaniment of wine. Great interchange of visiting takes place. It is called *'fadging,'* or 'eating *fadge.' Fadging* really means eating the bread of brotherly union and concord. 'Come and *fadge* with me' is as much as saying 'Come and break bread with me and taste wine, in token that bygones shall be bygones.' " – The Rev. J. W. Dunn, on Warkworth. *History of Berwickshire Naturalists' Club,* 1863, vol. v., p.56.

FAFF. To mess about.

FAGGIT. A term of contempt. *Ye impitent faggit.*

FAIR, FOR FAIR, FOR FAIRS. In earnest, seriously. See the Tyneside song – *Geordie Haad the Bairn. Haad the bairn for fairs, thou's often deun't for fun.*

FAIR-BEAT. Worn out.

FAIRIN. A present from a fair.

FAITHOR, FATHOR, FETHER. Father.

FALL, in the. In the autumn.

FAR-OWER. Much too. *Far-ower clivvor.*

FARD. Favoured. Especially in the expressions *ill-fard, well fard* – that is ugly-looking or good-looking.

FARDIN. Farthing.

FASH. Trouble. *Aa've hed a fashous job on't* – I've had a troublesome job with it.

FAWS. FAAS. The common name for a gypsy or tinker. Derived from Johnny Faw, a chief of the Scottish gypsies. Often used as a term of abuse. *Get oot, ye clarty Faa* – get out you dirty slut.

FELL. A hill. Used in numerous place names in Northumberland and Durham e.g. Low Fell, Gateshead Fell.

FELL. To knock down with a blow.

FEMMER. Weak, frail. *She's nobbut femmer, poor body* – She's frail, poor soul.

FENKLE. A bend or corner. A geographical term. There are Fenkle Streets in Newcastle and Alnwick. It has been suggested Finchdale (Abbey) is so called from a bend in the Wear at this point. This is very unlikely.

FERNIETICKLES. Freckles. *Rocket taketh away freckles on fayrntikles.* Turner of Morpeth, *Herbal,* 1551.

FETTLE. Good condition. *What fettle, marra?* Also used as a verb – to repair or put in order. *The lock wants fettlin.* Also to signify mood – *He's iv a bad fettle* – He's in a bad mood.

FEW. A small number. Used in expressions – *a good few* or *a cannv few* meaning a large number.

FEUL. A fool.

FEY.

"The word *fey* was formerly used both in Scotland and in the North of England to express the state of a person who was supposed to be dying but who would rise from his bed and go about the house, conversing with his friends, as if nothing ailed him. Persons also in health, whose eyes displayed unusual brightness, and who appeared to act and speak in a wild and mysterious manner when preparing for battle or for a perilous journey, were frequently said to be *'fey';* that is, doomed shortly to meet with their death." – S. Oliver, *Rambles in Northumberland,* 1835, p.108.

FINDY-KEEPY. Who finds keeps. A children's expression often used in more lengthy form – *lossy, seeky, findy, keepy.* When searching for something the child who says this claims right to keep the article.

FINNIE HADDIE. A finnan haddock, that is one cured with smoke derived from the village of Findon in Scotland.

FIT AS A LOP. Fit as a flea.

FLAAF. To fly about. *Reet fra the Spital to the clouds, it flaffered very suen, man.* Allan's *Tyneside Songs,* 1891.

FLAG. Flat sandstones used as roofing tiles. They were also used for paving, hence pavements were called *flags.*

FLAM. A lie.

FLAP. Trouser fly.

FLAPJACK. A small cake of flour fried in grease.

FLING. To throw.

FLIT. To remove from one house to another. Usually in the expression – *Moonlight flit,* when a tenant left with his household goods at night to avoid paying his rent. *And when we flit, the landlord stops ma sticks, till a' th' rent be paid.* Wilson, *The Pitman's Pay,* 1843.

FLUMMIX. To surprise. *He flummix'd him* – He had the best of the argument.

FLY-BY-NIGHT. See "Flit". A worthless person who gets into debt and then disappears to avoid paying.

FOIST. A damp and sour smell. The adjective is *foisty.* A *foisty room,* a *foisty loaf,* etc. It also means to pass something off as genuine.

FOLLY. Any ridiculous building. There are many examples in the north, e.g. Sharpe's Folly, Rothbury.

FOND. Half-witted, silly. *Fond as a besom* – daft as a brush.

FOOT. Lower part of a street as *head* the upper part. We still talk about the *head of the Side* and the *foot of the Side* in Newcastle.

FOOTRUNNER. Professional sprinter.

FORBY. In addition to, over and above. *He's sixteen stone onyway, forby the heavy side-saddle.*

FORE-SHIFT. The first shift of hewers who descend the pit for work.

FOR FAIRS. An expression which means "in earnest".

FORKYTAIL. Earwig.

FORNENST. Against, in front of.

FORST FOOT. The person who first enters a house on New Year's Day. A dark man is preferred and he brings in food or fuel, usually coal.

FOWERSOME. Four persons.

FOWT. Fought.

FOYBOATMAN. A boatman who watches for boats coming into the Tyne in the hope of getting employment in mooring them. The word foy means a fee or reward.

FRATCH. A quarrel, disagreement.

FRET. A fog on the coast usually called a *seafret.*

FROZZIN. Frozen.

FUNNIN. Joking.

FYUL. Fool.

G

GAAK. Stare.

GAB. Empty talk. Expression *gift of the gab* is common.

GADGIE. An old man employed as a watchman.

GAFF. A theatre or cinema. *Penny gaff* – cheap cinema matinee.

GAFFER. Foreman. Originally a term of respect for an old man.

GALLOWAY. A small horse originally from Galloway in Scotland. They were used to carry lead ore from the mines to the smelt mills. Pit ponies in Durham were always called *galloways.*

GALLUSES. Men's braces. Derived from the gallows on which people were hung.

GAMMY. Lame. *He's getten a gammy leg.*

GAN. To go. *As seun as aa hord him, aa gans up tiv him.*

GANNER. A good goer. *He's not bonny-leukin, but he's a ganner.*

GANNY. Grandmother.

GAN-ON. A fuss.

GANZIE. A thick woollen jersey, especially worn by fishermen. Said to originate from Guernsey.

GARTH. A guarded or fenced piece of ground. The old area covered by the castle was called the Castle Garth. *A tatie garth* – a potato field.

GATE. Occasionally it means gate in the modern sense. Newgate Street, Westgate Street and Gallowgate commemorate the old gates which led into the town. But usually it has the old Saxon meaning of a street or road. Narrowgate in Alnwick means a street not a town gate. The word also means the "manner of going on". *Gan yor ann gate – meant "go your own way".*

GAUMLESS. Silly, ignorant.

GAUP. To gape or stare. *What are ye gaupin at?* – What are you staring at?

GEE. Stubborness or taking the pique. *She teuk the gee* – She was very stubborn.

GEET. Great. *Geet big gob* – Great big mouth.

GEEZER. A mummer; and hence a queer character.

GEORDIE. See page 4

GETTEN. Got.

GEW-GAW. A Jew's,harp or mouth organ.

GEYEN. Gone.

GEYZENED. Dried up.

GI. To give.

GILL. A place hemmed in by two steep banks, usually wooded Although common in Cumberland it is rare in Northumberland. When pronounced with a soft g it means a half-pint.

GIMMER. A young ewe. Also a low woman.

GIRDLE, GORDLE. A flat circular iron plate with handle which is used on the open fire for making *singin-hinnies.* On any special occasion such as a birthday or wedding the *gordle was set* on for baking *spice singin-hinnies.* The cakes baked on the girdle were called *gordle-kyeks.*

GIRN. A fine Northumbrian word with several graduations of meaning. To gnash the teeth, to whimper, to show the teeth in laughing, to gape, to grin, etc. *Just like a monkey, he did gairn man.*

GISSY. A pig. For superstitious reasons, especially among fishermen, pigs were rarely called by their proper name.

GIVE-OWER. Give over. Stop.

GIZE. To disguise. Heslop tells the amusing story of a poacher who was not over clean, when going out on an expedition asked his wife, *Hoo mun a gize mesel? Wesh thee fyess,* was the prompt reply.

GIZER. A masquerader.

GLAIR. GLAUR. Mud, shining dirt, filth. Liquid mud more objectionable than *clarts*.

GLAKY. Slow witted.

GLASS ALLEY. A very fine playing marble.

GLEE-EYE. Squint eye.

GLIFF. A sudden fright. *He gave her such a gliff that she left the hoose.*

GLOWER. Glare. *He glowered at him* – He glared at him.

GOAF. The part of the mine from which all the coal has been worked.

GOB. The mouth. Often in the expression *gift o' the gab*. It is also to express insolence; *to set up his gob. A gobby brat* – an impudent child.

GOGGLEY or **GOOGLEY.** Staring eyes. In the song of the *Lambton Worm,* we have the worm described with *great big goggley eyes.*

GOLLAR. A growl.

"Between the Megstone Rock at the Farne Islands and the House Island, the opposite currents frequently cause a short, and to small boats a rather dangerous swell, like breakers. This ripple is known to the fishermen of the neighbourhood by the very significant name of the gollars" – S. Oliver, *Rambles in Northumberland,* 1835, p.204.

GOLLUP. To gulp one's food, *Dinna gollup your food like that.*

GONIEL. A fool, stupid person.

GOOD FEW. A fair number, *A canny few.*

GOOSE'S FLESH. The feeling on the skin when cold or afraid because it was thought it was like a plucked fowl.

GORD. Metal hoop. *The bairns hez all getten gords ti play wi'. The gords is aall comin' off the rain tubs.*

GOWK. The heart of a plant, especially of an apple. Also means a simpleton: *April gowk* – April fool. *Ye're a gowk if ye don't know that the lads i' Tyneside are the Jacks that myek famish wor Navy.* Song. *Canny Newcassel.*

GOWSTY. Gusty. *Gan roon' the corner; it's ower gowsty here.*

GOX. A common oath. A corruption of God.

GRAFFLIN. Searching for something with one's hand.

GRAYNE. A clan or family.

GREEDY HOUND. One who bolts his meat like a dog.

GREET. To cry.

GREY HEN. A large stone-ware bottle, usually containing intoxicating liquor.

GRIPE. A garden fork.

GROOP. A drain or ditch. In Newcastle the *Javel Groop* was a narrow opening leading from the Close to the river. Originally it was the *Gaole Grippe* – the gaol ditch. Javel is a corruption of gaol.

GROSSER. A gooseberry. *On beef an' grosser dumplings they varra fain wad feed.* Chatt. 1866.

GRUMLE. To grumble. In many similar words: stumble, rumble, jumble the b is silent.

GRUNSTON. Grindstone. See the famous proverb – *A Scot, a rat, and a Newcastle grunston are found in every part of the world.*

GUESS. Now considered an Americanism, but in a Newcastle book of 1686 we read: *I guess they've heard what this day's vote is.*

GUESSING-STORY. A conundrum or riddle. The winter nights in many country houses were passed by the fire light and *guessing-stories* often relieved the graver talk. The *guessing-stories* had a narrative form, and were not mere puzzles in a sentence. Such a one as the following is a common instance. "Clink, clank doon the bank, ten again fower, splish, splash in the dish, till it run ower." Answer, the milking of a cow. Both hands are required – that is, ten fingers against the four teats. Another: "As green as grass, as white as milk and bearded like a pard." Answer, a turnip." Heslop.

GUILD-BELL. The bell (the great bell of St. Nicholas' church) which summons the meeting of the Newcastle freemen.

GULLY. A large knife.

GUTSTY. Gluttonous.

GYEP. Gape.

GYET. A gate. A street.

GYETSID. Gateshead.

GYEZEND. Parched. *Gi's a drink I'm gyezend* – Give me a drink I'm thirsty.

H

HAAD. Hold. *Haad yer gob* – Hold your mouth. *Haad yor whisht* – has the same meaning.

HAAD ON. Hold back. *Haad on a min't* – wait a moment.

HAAK. A hawk. Also to cough.

HAAKER. Hawker.

HACKY. Tyneside slang for dirty. *Hacky-dorty* – means "very dirty".

HADAWAY. Begone. *Hadaway wi' ye.* Also used as a term of encouragement. *Howay the lads* is a corruption of Hadaway.

HADDER-UP. A holder up. A plater's helper in the shipyard. Trade now obsolete.

HADDIN. Holding. *He was haddin on for bare life.*

HAG; HAGG; PEAT-HAG; or **MOSS-HAG.** "A projecting mass of peat forming an escarpment on a peat moor, or the peat on high moors left by edges of water gutters. These hags form miniature ravines on the surface." Heslop.

HAGGISMEAT. On Tyneside means minced pieces of tripe.

HAGGER'T. Beggared.

HALE. The goal at football.

"Rothbury, the custom of football-play on Shrove Tuesday had been observed from time immemorial until the year 1867. The *hale* or goal of the Thropton men was the bridge over the Wreigh at Thropton." – D. D. Dixon, *Shrowe-tide Customs,* p.3.

HALF-COCKED. Half drunk.

HALFERS.

"A cry amongst children claiming half of anything that has been given or found. When an article has been lost, a lad guards against the claim of sharing by calling out, *No halfers; lossie, findie, seekie, keepie.* If he finds it after this he is supposed to be its individual owner." Heslop.

HALF-NOWT. Almost nothing.

HAM. Anglo-Saxon word used as an ending in place names. Common in Northumberland as *Ovingham, Whittingham* etc.

HAME. Home.

HAMMER. To strike in a fight. To give a thorough beating to an opponent. *Aa'll hammer ye* – I'll give you a good hiding.

HAND-PUTTER. Colliery term. One who *puts* without the help of a pony.

HANG-FIRE. Wait.

HANSTORN. Work. *I havn't deun a hanstorn the day.* I haven't done any work today.

HAP. An overcoat or extra covering. To cover. *Hap weel up; it's a caad neet* – Wrap yourself up, it's a cold night. There is a famous Newcastle saying which tells us: *At the Westgate came Thornton in, with a hap, a halfpenny and a lambskin.* Another version reads: *At the West Gate came Thornton in, with a happen hapt in a ram's skynne.*

HAP-PAST. Half-past.

HARD CARD. Poverty.

HARDLIES. Hardly.

HARLE. A heronry.

HARR. A mist.

HARRIN. The herring. *Caller harrin* – Fresh herring. A local street call no longer heard.

HASTY PUDDING. Oatmeal porridge.

HAUGH. A geographical term found often in Northumberland but rarely in Durham. A flat piece of land on a riverside.

HAWKIE. A white faced cow.

HEATHER-BUZZOM. A besom made of heather.

HECKLER. A sharp tongued woman.

HEE. High. The place name *Healey* means a "high clearing".

HEED. Head.

HELP. Fill.

HEMMEL. A cattle shed.

"An outbuilding on a farm; in olden days made of upright posts, with whin or broom interlaced, and a thatched roof, chiefly used in winter and the lambing season. The permanent hemmel, which forms a conspicuous feature in Northumberland farm buildings, is surrounded by a fold yard, and has in front an arcade of massive masonry, frequently surmounted by a granary. The *hemmel-eye* is the archway orifice giving access to the covered arcade. Four inhabited and four uninhabited place-names in Northumberland occur in combination with hemmel. Example, Red *Hemmels.*" Heslop.

HEOR. Here.

HET. An exclamation of impatience *Het ! haud yur tongue.*

HET. Hat.

HEUGH. A precipitous hill or cliff.

HEUK-NEBBED. Hook-nosed.

HEW. To dig coal. Noun is *Hewer.*

HEYEM. Home. *They hed sic a heyem-coming as nivvor was.*

HEZ. Has. *He hez nowt.*

HIND. Farm servant hired by the year. He usually had to provide a female worker called a bondager.

HINNY. Local pronunciation of "honey". A favourite term of endearment applied usually to women and children. Often used together with the similar word *canny.*

Where hest te been, ma canny hinney?
An' where hest te been, ma bonny bairn?
Aw was up and doon seekin' for ma hinney;
Aw was thro' the toon seekin' for ma bairn.
                    (from The Collier's Pay Week.)

HINTEND. Posterior.

HIP. To hop. HIPPIN-STONES are stepping stones across a stream.

HIPPINS. Nappies.

HIRING. A fair where servants were hired.

HIRSEL. Stock of sheep belonging to a hill farmer. The shepherd's portion which he grazed in return for his work is called a "pack".

HIRST. A wood or thicket. Used as part of place name in *Longhirst.*

HIT. It. Once common as in – *That's hit noo.*

HITCH. To hop on one leg.

HITCHY-DABBER. A children's game in which the players hop over lines "skotched on the ground". Hence the other name Hop Scotch.

HITTY-MISSY. At random.

HOASTMEN. The old word, now obsolete, to describe a coal-shipper at Newcastle.

HOB. Iron pin used in playing quoits. Also describes the iron bars in front of a fire. *Put the kettle on the hob.*

HOGGERS. Footless stockings worn by pitmen at work. In olden times the pitman wore his stockings with the feet cut off so when small coals got into the stocking foot he only pulled off the foot and not the whole stocking.

HOIT. A contemptible person. *Ye greet lazy hoit.*

HOITY-TOITY. Flighty, assuming airs.

HOLEY-STONE. A stone with a hole in it (natural not artificial) which was thought to have magic properties.

HONKERS. Haunches. Especially in the expression *sittin on his honkers.*

HONOUR BRIGHT. A phrase in which children express their honour. The Newcastle worthy here commemorated is now unknown.

HOOKY. Truancy.

HOOKY-MAT. A mat made from rags and clippings.

HOOND. A hound or a low fellow.

HOOND-TRAIL. A drag hunt.

HOOSE. House.

HOPPINS. An annual festival. Hopping or dancing was the main amusement, hence the name. In Newcastle the Easter *hoppin* was the most famous but it was replaced in 1882 by the Temperance Festival on the Town Moor which takes place in Race Week. Known as *The Hoppins* it is claimed to be the largest in the world.

HORSE-STYEN. Local name for a mounting stone, for mounting a horse.

HOT-TROD. A Border custom in which a wisp of straw or tow was set on fire and carried on a spear as a signal to every man to follow in pursuit of thieves and marauders.

HOUGH. The back of the knee. The expression *cruck yor hough* means to sit down.

HOUGHER. Public whipper or executioner in Newcastle. The name originates from one of his early functions which was to cut the houghs of swine which roamed the streets of the town. In 1827 he was receiving a yearly salary of £4.6s.8d.

HOULET. The owl.

HOUSIN. The capability of holding a lot, as, *He has a good housin* for drink.

HOW. A salutation. Especially in *How there, marra?* followed by the reply *What cheer, hinney.*

HOWDY. A midwife.

HOWK. To dig. *He's howkin taties* – He's digging up potatoes.

HOWKY. The old name for a pitman.

HOY. To throw. *To hoy a stone* – To throw a stone.

HOY-OOT. Still sometimes heard at Tyneside weddings. The wedding couple are supposed to throw coppers to the boys and girls who are calling. The tradition however may be derived from the song of the famous Geordie comedian, Harry Nelson.

> *Hi, Canny Man, Hoy a Ha'penny Oot,*
> *Ye'll see some fun thor is nee doot,*
> *Where ivvor aa gan ye'll hear them shoot,*
> *Hi, Canny Man, hoy a ha'penny oot!*

HOYIN OOT TIME. Closing time for a pub.

HOYIN SKYUL. A gathering to play pitch and toss.

HUCKSTER. A small tradesman.

HUDDOCK. The cabin of a keel boat.

HUFF. To offend. *He's tyen the huff.* He is offended.

HULLABALOO. A tumult.

HULE-DOO. A figure made of gingerbread or dough and rolled flat. Currants are used for eyes. Specially made at Xmas, hence the name *Yule.*

HUMP. Temper. *He's getten his hump up* – He's in a bad temper. It also means to "carry".

HUNK. A large piece. *A hunk o' breed.*

HUNKERS. Haunches. Only used in the sense of sitting on the hunkers. It is a favourite resting position among the northern miners. *Aa teuk the chance to sit doon on me hunkers to leet me pipe.*

HUT. A heap. *A muck hut* is a heap of manure. Also used as a verb – *We've hutten wor tormits* (turnips).

HUTCH. A treasure chest, usually applied to the town treasure chest, as at Morpeth and Newcastle, called *the toon hutch.*

HUZZY. Abbreviated form of "housewife." Not always a term of reproach except when an adjective is added as in *brazen huzzy.*

HYEM. Home. *I'm gannin hyem.*

I

I. In. Used before consonant. Before a vowel it becomes *iv. Where i' the warld are ye gannin? Aa's iv a horry.*

IDLE. Immoral. *An idle huzzy* – an immoral woman.

IMP. A mischievous child.

INATWEEN. Between.

IN-BYE. Within. Mining term meaning in the workings of a pit, inward from the shaft.

INSIGHT. Household goods.

INTAKE. Land taken in and fenced.

INSTEED. Instead.

IVVOR. Ever.

J

JAA. The jaw. Verb – "to talk".

JAA-BREAKER. A long word.

JACK. A coat of armour (16th century) made by sewing iron plates to a riding coat.

JARP. To strike. Jarping eggs at Easter is a north country custom. One holds an egg and challenges anyone to strike it with another egg. The first broken egg is the spoil of the conqueror.

JARRA. The town of Jarrow.

JEDDART LAA. Jedburgh justice, meaning "hang first, try afterwards." The kind of rough justice prevalent on both sides of the Border.

JOWL. To strike a wall in a coal pit as a signal. When pitmen are imprisoned by an accident they jowl to show their position to the rescuers.

JUGGERY POKERY. Underhand dealing. Trickery.

JONTY. John.

K

KEEK. Soup eaten by poor people. *He was browt up on keek.*

KEEK. To peep. *I just took a keek in ti' find oot what was on.*

KEEKER. Overlooker at a pit whose main job is to examine the coals as they come out of a pit.

KEEL. A large boat for carrying coal on the Tyne. It is the first English word to be written down (by Gildas the 6th century British historian).

KEEL-BULLY. A comrade on a keel.

KEEL-DEETER. A keel cleaner. A privilege of the wives and daughters of keelmen who kept the sweepings for their fires.

KEEL ROW. The internationally known Tyneside Song. It first appears in written form in a manuscript book of 1774 belonging to the Newcastle Society of Antiquaries.

KEN. To know, to remember.

KEP. To catch something falling.

KEPPY BA'. Handball. A ball that is thrown and caught. A ball for bouncing is called a *stotty-baal.*

KERN. The end of harvest, celebrated with a *Kern-supper.*

KID. A child.

KIDDAR. A friendly term of address applied to children. The word is now known worldwide because the famous Newcastle writer Jack Common used it in the title of his first book – *Kiddar's Luck.* The word is also slang for one guilty of a *leg pull.*

KIDDY. A son, a native. *Show what noted kiddies fre Newcastle toon hes flit.* W. Armstrong, 1825.

KIPPER. A kipper was once a smoked or dried salmon. In tne 18th century it was used in the north for a *kippered herring.* Recently it has come into general use nationally.

KIST; CIST. "A box or chest. A *deputy's kist* is the chest used by the deputy in a coal pit, wherein he keeps his tools, plate nails, brattice nails, and other requirements. *Coffin kist,* a hearse. Prehistoric burials are sometimes found in regularly made boxes of stone, four or more of which are set on edge, whilst one or more form a close cover or lid. These are known as *kists* by the country people and as *cists* by the archeologist." Heslop.

KITE. The stomach, belly. *A pain in the kyte.*

KITTLE. Tickle.

KITTY. A prison. Also a common fund or pool in some games.

KIZZEN. To dry up by overcooking. *She's kizzened the pot.*

KNACKERS. Two flat pieces of stone. or hard wood charred at the ends and used as castanets.

KNACKERED. Tired, worn out.

KNAKKY-KNEED. Knock-kneed.

KNEDDING CAKE. A cake kneaded with lard or butter and baked on a girdle.

KNOOLED. Dispirited.

KYE. Cow, kine.

KYEK. Cake.

KYEL. Soup, broth. In the 18th century they often put raisins in the broth which was then called *spice-kyel.*

L

LAA. Low. *He wis varry laa doon* – He was in very low spirits.

LACE. To mix spirits with tea. Also to "thrash". *Aall lace ye* – I'll give you a good hiding.

LAD. A sweetheart. *She wis gan a waak wiv her lad* – she was out walking with her sweetheart.

LADS. A group of comrades, not always young people. *Haaks's lads,* etc.

LADS-ALIVE. An exclamation like *man-alive.*

LAID-IN. Mining term meaning a colliery has ceased working because the coal is exhausted.

LAIDLEY. Loathsome. See *The Laidley Worm of Spindleston Heugh.*

LAIRD. A landowner living upon and cultivating his own land. Once used in North Northumberland.

LAITH. Loth, unwilling. *Aa wad be laith ti gan win him* – I wouldn't go with him.

LANG. Long.

LANG-LAST. At last.

LANG-NEB. A prominent nose. *Keep yor lang-neb oot o' this* – mind your own business.

LANG SYNE. Long since, long ago.

LARN. To teach, to learn.

LASHINS. Plenty. *Lashins o' meat and drink* – Plenty of food and drink.

LASS. A sweetheart. *Wor lass* however means "my wife".

LAST BAT. A game of tiggy. When children are parting on their way home they try to give a *bat* without being touched.

LAVEROCK. Skylark. More common across the Border.

LAVVY. Lavatory.

LEAZES. Stinted grass pastures. Found in most Northumbrian towns: Castle-Leazes at Newcastle, Shaftoe-Leazes at Hexham, Heather-Leazes at Warkworth.

LEISH. Lithe, full of youthful vigour. *Whas like ma Johnnie, sae leish, sae blithe, sae bonnie.*

LEISTER. A salmon spear used by poachers.

LICK. A small quantity. *A lick and a promise,* local saying. Also applied to a cursory wash.

LIFT. To steal. Euphemism for theft when applied to cattle rustling on the Border. Still in general use today.

LIFTIN. Moving with life, full of, *His claes wis liftin wi' varmin.*

LININS. Underpants.

LINKS. Sandy grass covered land near the sea shore. E.g. Blyth Links, Whitley Links. Now often applied to golf courses.

LINN. Strictly the deep pool at the base of a waterfall but sometimes applied to the cascade itself.

LINTIE. The willow wren. Used on Tyneside to describe someone who is quick – *as active as a lintie.*

LIST. Vigour, energy. The expression *Aa henna the list to dee'd* – I haven't the energy to do it.

LOAD. As much as can be carried on the back of a pack-horse. Used in the expressions – *Loads o' money, loads o' time. He taaks a reet load* – He talks nonsense (a load of rubbish).

LOANIN, LONNEN. Originally a sheltered place where cows were gathered for milking. Now used for a lane or narrow road.

LOLLY. The tongue. *Oppen thy gob hinny and put out thy lolly.*

LOOPY. Insane, daft.

LOP. A flea. *The penny lop* was the local cinema which was full of people with fleas. *Fit as a lop.*

LOUGH. A lake. All the loughs in Northumberland are small.

LOWE. A light.

LOWP. To leap, jump. *When aa wes yung an lusty, aa cud lowp the dyke.* (Sair fyeld Hinny). A *louping-on-stane* was slang for a mounting block for horsemen.

LOWSE. Finishing time. *Howway lads, it's lowse* – Time gentlemen.

LUG. Ear.

LUM. Chimney.

M

MAAKY. Maggoty.

MAIMY. Diminutive of "Mary".

MAD-HET. Very hot.

MAIR. More.

MAN. A husband.

MARROW. A comrade, a work-mate. *We've been working marrows for the last six months.* Also to match, to equal.

> *Bout Lunnen then divent ye myek sic a rout. There's nowse there maw winkers to dazzle, For aw the fine things ye are gobbin about, We can marra in Canny Newcassell.* Song, Canny Newcassell.

> "Newcassell 'ill nivor find owt like its *marrow*" (find anything like its equal). – *Joe Wilson's Songs. – Allan's Collection, 1890, p. 185.*

> "Ev'ry of them beside her *Marrow*
> Walks e'en as strait as ev'r was arrow."
> G. Stuart, *Joco-Serious Discourse,* 1686, p. 12.

> "As me and my *marrow* was gannin to wark."
> The Colliers Rant. – Bell's Rhymes, 1812, p. 35.

> "Ho ! *marrows,* 'tis the caller cries;
> And his voice in the gloom of the night mist dies."
> Edward Corvan, d. 1865, *The Caller.*

MASK. To infuse tea. *Wor lass's ganna mask the tye* (tea).

MAYBIES, MEVVIES. Perhaps. *Maybies aa wull gan* – Perhaps I will go.

MAZER. A wonder, an eccentric. Well known word from Tommie Armstrongs famous Song – *Wor Nannie's a mazor.*

MEG. A halfpenny.

MEGGIE. Margaret.

MELL. A wooden mallet as used by masons.

MICKLE. Means "much not little" as is often thought. Mickle and muckle mean the same. The well known saying *Many a* *mickle makes a muckle* is a misquotation. It should be *Many a pickle makes a muckle.*

MIDDEN. A dunghill or heap. The "Black Middens" were dangerous rocks near Tynemouth pier.

MIND. A word with many meanings. *Mind me on* – Bid me remember, *Mind ye dinna stop ower lang* – Be sure you don't stop too long, *Aa've a good mind ti clash yor jaa* – I feel like hitting you on the chin.

MISDOOT. To doubt, to suspect. *Ye mevvies misdoot me* – You perhaps doubt me.

MISTRESS. Mrs.

MIZZLE. Fine rain. Also used in slang for to "disappear".

MOONGIN. Moaning, grumbling. *He's elwis gan moongin aboot* – He's always going around grumbling.

MOOT. A meeting. Hence MOOT HALL, Newcastle, where the Assizes are held.

MORN. Morrow, morning. *He'll be there the morn.*

MORTALIOUS. Mortal drunk. Everybody who attends the Newcastle court and for that matter other police courts in the north, is familiar with the finely expressive word 'mortalious'."
Newcastle Evening Chronicle, Aug. 8th, 1898.

MOSS TROOPER. A Border raider accustomed to cross the mosses of the march lands.
Moss-troopers: that is thieves and robbers, who, after having committed offences in the Borders, do escape through wastes and mosses." *Statute of Charles II.*

MOTE HILLS. Hills with earthen ramparts. Derived from *motte and bailey* castle. Origin of the word forgotten in the Middle Ages.
"The inhabitants of Redesdale and Tindale, accustomed to have their disputes settled, and themselves to sit as jurymen, upon the mote-hills at Harbottle or Elsdon, and at Wark or Haltwhistle." Hodgson's *Northumberland.*

MOUNTIEKITTIE. A children's game meaning "Mount the cuddie." The players mount each other's backs shouting out *Montiekittie, Montiekittie, one, two, three.*

MOW. Moment. *Haad on a mow* – wait a moment.

MUCK. Dirt, manure. *There's nout like muck.* James Pigg speaking in favour of manure as a fertilizer. Also means to "bungle a job. *He's mucked the job up.*

MUG. Face, Fool. A drinking vessel.

MUGGER. In the North of England was applied to a tinker or travelling hawker. When describing hard work there is a common saying, *Aa's sweetin like a mugger's cuddy.*

MUGGLES. Marbles.

MY EYE. Slang expression for *nonsense, rubbish.*

N

NA. No.

NAG. To worry with fault-finding. *What are ye naggin on at ?*

NARKT. Annoyed. *He was very narkt* – He was very annoyed.

NATTER. To gossip in an unfriendly way.

NEB. Nose. *Wet yor neb* – take a drink.

NECK. Impudence. *What a neck ye hev.*

NEE. No. *I hev nee tatties* – I have no potatoes.

NETTIE. Lavatory. For further details about this famous Geordie word see *The Geordie Nettie* by Frank Graham.

NEUK. A nook.

NEWCASSELL. Usually in form *Canny Newcastle.*

NICK. A notch. A mark usually made on a stick. Often made to facilitate reckoning. The old expression – *she has lost her nick-stick* meant a person had lost her reckoning of time.

NIGH. Near, almost. *Aa wis nigh lossin me hat.* I almost lost my hat.

NIP. A pinch. It was once customary to give a person a nip when he first appeared in new clothes, calling out *nip for new*. It also means a small quantity.

NOBBUT. Only. *Aa's nobbut badly thi day.*

NOODLE. Yeomanry, cavalry. A term of abuse because the local yeomanry were intensely disliked.

NOWT. Nothing. In the trial scene of Surtees *Handley Cross* we read: First you have James Pigg, the huntsman, who informs us in his subterranean language – if, indeed, it can be called a language – that he said *nout*, which, I suppose, is meant to imply that he did not warrant the horse; the word *nout* doubtless being one of extensive signification in the colliery country, from which this witness comes."

NUMB. Stupid.

NYEM. Name. A Tynesider says *Aa divvent knaa his nyem.*

O

OASTE. Name given to a person who came to Newcastle to buy coal. The vendor was called a *hoastman.*

OILIN HIS WIG. A slang expression meaning he is "Drinking heavily".

ON-PUT The overlay of beds, above an outcrop – mining term.

OOT-BACK. Outside lavatory.

OOT BYE. Outside. *It's varra caad oot bye* – It's very cold outside. Also a mining term meaning "towards the bottom of the pit shaft."

OWER. *He hes far ower much ti say for hissell.*

OXTERS. Armpits. "My coat is tight under the oxters."

PAAKY. Conceited. Choosy about food.

PAANSHOP. Pawn Shop. See the book – *A Lang Way to the Panshop* by Thomas Callaghan.

PALLATIC. Corruption of paralytic, meaning "very drunk".

PAN. A salt pan. See place-name of *Howdon Pans*.

PANHAGGERTY, PANHAGGLETY. Is a dish containing potatoes, onions and grated cheese. A traditional Northumbrian dish which is still popular. The name is peculiar to Tyneside. Sometimes left-over meat was used.

PANT. A public water fountain.

PARKIN. A northern cake made of treacle and oatmeal.

PARNICKETY. Fastidious.

PAST. To be "past oneself" means to be distracted. *Thor's myekin sic a noise aa's fair past mesel.*

PASTE EGG. A hard boiled Easter egg. The "boolin" and "jaapin" of Easter eggs was a very old northern custom.

PAY. To thrash. *Aa'll pay yor hide* – I'll give you a good hiding.

PEASE PUDDIN. A pudding made from split peas flavoured with ham. Can be eaten hot or cold.

"Pease puddin hot, pease puddin cold.
Pease puddin in the pot, nine days old."

(North Country Rhyme).

PELE. A tower. A Border term.

PELT. To hurry along. *Full pelt* – full speed.

PENNY-STANE. A quoit.

PETH. A path. Occurs in several place names as *Morpeth*.

PETTING-STONE.

PETTING-STONE. A custom prevails at Bamburgh and other places, on the occasion of a wedding, for the bride to be lifted over a stone, called the *petting-stone,* at the church gates after the ceremony. It is generally commuted by a money payment. There is a stone in the churchyard at Holy Island where the same ceremony is practised. It is the socket stone of a Saxon cross. At Ford, a "paten-stick" was used. It was placed before the church door when the bride and bridegroom came out, and the newly-wedded ones had to "loup" it, or else pay the usual fine. A similar custom prevailed in many Northumberland villages.

"Being here (at Shilbottle) one day while a pitman's wedding was going on, we were amused with the custom of lifting the ladies over a heap of stones laid in the middle of the footpath." – Correspondent in the *Alnwick Mercury,* July 15th, 1861.

PICKLE. A small quantity. *Gi's a pickle mair* – Give me a little more.

PIG PIGGY. An earthenware hot water bottle. Heslop tells us that a traveller in Northumberland was astonished when told that country people slept with the *pigs* for warmth.

PIGGIN. An earthenware pitcher.

PIKE. A small pointed stack of hay containing about one cartload. It is erected temporarily awaiting transport to the farm yard.

PIKE. A pointed hill. The opposite is *Dodd,* a truncated hill.

PILLAR. A mining term for the square masses of coal left in a working to support the roof.

PIN. Humour. *A jug o' Geordy's maut an' hop suin put us in a merry pin.* T. Wilson. *Pitman's Pay.*

PIN-WELL. A well where native offerings were made. In the 19th century valuable gifts were replaced by pins.

"A curious custom was long observed in connection with a well at the foot of Horsedean, near Wooler. On May-day a procession was formed and marched from the town (Wooler) to this spot, where a halt was called, and each of the processionists dropped a crooked pin into it, at the same time 'wishing a wish.' Though the formal procession on May-day morning is no longer acted, the custom is still kept up by young people." – James Hall, *Guide to Glendale,* 1887, p.9.

"About a mile west of Jarrow, their is a well still called Bede's Well to which, as late as the year 1740, it was a prevailing custom to bring diseased children; a crooked pin was put into the well, which was lewed dry between each dipping of the patient. But on every midsummer-eve there was a great resort of neighbouring people, with bonfires, music and dancing, to St. Bede's Well." – *Impartial History of Newcastle,* 1801.

PIT. A colliery.

PITCH-AN'-TOSS. "A gambling game, formerly in general use in the district. The players, who are called a *school,* place a bit of white *boody* (the *mot*) in position. This is aimed at by each in succession, the first player having the choice of the place (*the past*) from which to pitch. Pence and halfpence are used as quoits. The player whose coin lies nearest to the *mot* then picks up the whole of the coins, and, laying them on his hand, tosses them up with a spin. All that come down lying head up become his own; the tails pass on to the next player, who tosses again, leaving the tails for the next in succession. The process is repeated till all the coins are disposed of." Heslop.

PITMATIC. The northern coal miners had certain words and expressions peculiar to themselves, which were called *pitmatic.*

PITTLE. To urinate.

PIT-YAKKOR. A term of abuse applied to pitmen.

PLASH. A downpour of rain.

PLATER. A shipyard term meaning a man who puts on shipplates.

PLOAT. To pluck out the feathers of a bird. When it snowed children used to sing various local rhymes similar to the following:

The aad wives' i' the east they're ploatin their geese,
An' sendin a' the white feathers ti me.

PLODGE. To wade in water with bare feet. *Along the sand we myed wor way, like plodgers on a rainy way.* Wilson, *Tyneside Songs,* 1890.

PLOWD. To *plodge* in dirt. *Plodge* is usually used for wading in water; *plowd* for wading in mud. *He's been plodging i' the wetter aall day, and now he's plowdin through the clarts.*

PLUFF. To spit. A *pluffer* was a tube used as a pea-shooter.

PLUFF. A plough. The many Plough Inns of the area were often pronounced as *Pluff Inn.*

POKE-HORSE. A pack-horse. So named because it carried bags on top of its saddle. A POKE-PUDDIN was a pudding boiled in a bag. The proverb *Mair poke nor puddin* means "more show than substance."

POKY. Inquisitive.

POSEY. Decorated with flowers. Mackenzie tells us that the pitmen's holiday waistcoats (called by them *posey* jackets) were frequently of very curious patterns, displaying flowers of various dyes."

POSS. To wash clothes by beating them in a *poss-tub* filled with hot water. The instrument used is a *poss-stick* a heavy piece of wood with a stalk and heavy foot.

POT. Usually used in the expression *gan te pot* – meaning one is "in a mess."

POT LUCK. The chance of the table.

POT-PIE. A pie made of beef chopped into pieces surrounded by dough and then boiled in a pot.

PROG. To prick. *Aa've prog'd me thoom wiv a needle* – I've pricked my thumb with a needle. A *proggy* mat receive's its name from the method used in making it.

PUT. A word with many meanings and often used. Here is Heslop's full explanation.

PUT. To palpitate, to throb; as in the sensation when an abscess is forming and the pulsations are felt in the inflamed part. "Me hand's *puttin'*, an' aa's flaid it's gan ti beeld." "A *puttin'* pain" – pain felt at each pulsation. *Put*, to vegetate, as when a plant begins to show the first sign of buds. "Aa see it's aall reet; it's *puttin.*" *Put*, to push, to thrust forward. To *put* a stone is to thrust it forward. In doing this the hand is held up over the shoulder and the stone is laid on the flat palm. A slight bending of the knees and a quick recovery of the upright position enables the thrower to *put* the stone forward with great force. To *put* a tram is to propel it. To propel a keel with a powey is called to *put* or to set. To *put* the door or to *put to* the door is to push it close. *"Put* the door." "See that the door's *put to." Put-back*, to thrust or hold back. *Put-down*, to put to death. A horse or dog are said to be *put-down* – they are not said to be killed or destroyed. To *put oneself doon* is to commit suicide. *Put-on*, dressed. To *put-on*, in mining, is to overlie. The *on-put* is the overlay of beds, etc., above an outcrop. See ON-PUT. *Put-out*, to crop out. "The limestone *puts-out." Put-ower*, to tide over, to survive. "Aa'll try to *put-ower* till Christmas." "He'll not *put-ower* the neet" (said of one in the last extremity). *Put-pay*, the payment of the fortnight's wages delayed until after the usual day. – *Nicholson. Putter*, in mining, the man who conveys coal from the hewer to the flat. The *putters* put or push the tram forward from behind. *Putter* has become applied to anyone who conveys the coal from the face to the flat – or station whence it is hauled by engine-power. Hence *hand-putter* and *pony-putter*, the latter being the lad who drives where ponies are used in bringing out the coal from the working place to the flat. *Putters* are also called *barrowmen. Put-through*, to get through with effort. "If aa oney *put-through* this job aa'll be reet eneuf." *Puttin-hewer*, in mining, a young hewer who is liable to be called upon to put if necessary. *Puttin-ponies*, ponies ten or eleven hands high, used in substitution for putters or barrowmen.

"I have heard of Iron Frames that have been used to *put back* these Quick Sands." – J. C., *Compleat Collier*, 1708, p. 21.

"May, 1589. Alice Stokoe, the 13 May buried. She was servant to Thomas Hodgson, butcher, and did *put down* herselfe in her maistor's house in her own belt." – Brand, *Hist. of Newcastle*, vol. i., p. 674.

"1564. This yeare Partrage was *put downe* for coyninge fals monnye in the Great Innes in Pilgrame Street." – *Carr MS*. – R. Welford, *Hist. of Newcastle in XVI. Century*, p. 397.

"He likes to see ye weel *put on*." – James Horsley, *A New Start for '81*.

PYET. Head.

R

RAA. A row of houses. *The Pit Raa.*

RAAF. Timber, but later "odds and ends." A Raaf yaird was originally a timber yard.

RAG. To tease, also to scold. *He got a rare raggin ower the job* – He was severely scolded for his work.

RAIM. To talk or call fretfully. *He just raimed away like one oot iv his heed.*

RANDY. A disorderly, scolding, quarrelsome woman. *She's a reg'lar randy.*

RANT. A lively song with chorus.

RAPPER. A knocker. A term also used down the mines.

REAVE. To rob. Specially used in connection with the **Border** raiders.

> "The limmer thieves o' Liddesdale
> Wad na leave a kye in the hail countrie:
> But an we gie them the caud steel,
> Our gear they'll *reive* it a' awaye."
>
> *The Fray o' Hautwessell.*

REDE. Counsel. Usually used in the proverb: *Short rede is good rede.* This proverb has become famous from the story of the murder of Bishop Walcher at Gateshead in 1080. The Norman bishop had just met the leaders of the local Saxons and made exorbitant demands for money from them. When he returned to the church to await their reply the cry was raised – *Shorte rede, good rede, slay ye the bishop.* The crowd set fire to the church and the bishop was slain.

REED. Pronunciation of red. *Reedhot* – red-hot.

REEK. Smoke. *The chimleys reekin badly.*

REET. Right. Used in many expressions. *Not reet iv his head.*

REEVE. The chief officer at Warkworth and elsewhere.

RIDING-THE-STANG. Carrying a man astride a pole. Generally a punishment for a faithless husband, but among miners was a sign of triumph.

RIG. A ridge.

RIVE. A rent in a garment.

ROLLEY. A carriage used down the pit.

ROONDY. Large coal.

ROUT. To roar. *Routing-Linn* – the roaring Linn – a waterfall.

ROWAN-TREE. The mountain ash. A tree often occuring in northern folklore.

ROWLY-POWLY. Rolling over and over. Also a game of chance.

ROZZEL. To heat over a fire. *Rozzel yor shins.*

RUBBIN-STYEN. A soft stone used for rubbing on door-steps and floors. A common practice fifty years ago.

RUNT. A small ox or cow.

S

SACKLESS. Useless, simple, stupid. *He's a greet sackless cuddy* – He's a big stupid donkey.

SAD. Bad. *He's iv a sad way.*

SAINT CUTHBERT'S BEADS. The name of the encrinites – fossilized sea animals – found on the sands of Holy Island.

ST. CUTHBERT'S DUCKS. Eider Ducks.

SANG. Song. *To myek a song* – To make a great outcry.

SARK. A shirt. *When I cam to Walker wark I had ne coat ne pit sark.* Bell's *Rhymes of the Bard.* 1812.

SCABBY. Shabby. *A scabby fellow.*

SCAD. To Scald. *Scaddin het* – Scalding hot.

SCALLION. A Scottish and Northumbrian word meaning "spring onion."

SCONCE. A seat at the side of an old chimney.

SCONE. A thick round cake baked on a girdle.

SCOOR. To rub clean.

SCOOT. To squirt.

SCORE. A standard number of tubs of coal upon which putters wages are based. In Durham a score is twenty-one tubs, in Northumberland twenty.

SCOTCH DRAPER. An itinerant seller of goods on credit. Also called a *manadge-man* or *ticket man.*

SCOTCH MIST. A sea fret.

SCRAN. Food.

SCRANCHUM. The hard skin or "crackling" of roast pork. Also gingerbread baked in thin wafers. All so called because they *scranch* or crackle in eating.

SCRAT. To scratch, like a rag collector on a rubbish heap. Hence the expression *to scrat for a leevin* – to make a precarious living.

SCRIBE. Handwriting. *Just gi'z a bit scribe off yor han to show whe aa is.*

SCRIMP. To shorten, to act like a miser. *The aad miser's as scrimpy as can be.*

SCRUFF. Nape of the neck. *He tyuk him bi the scruff o' the neck.*

SCRUFFY. Dirty.

SCUILL. School.

SCUMFISH. To choke with smoke. *The chimley's been smokin' till aa's fair scumfished.*

SCUNNER. A Tyneside word with many meanings. Best described in a few of its uses. *He's tyen a scunner at her* – He's taken an aversion to her. *She's gotten the scunners* – She's taken the huff. *He didn't scunner me at all* – He didn't notice me.

SEA COAL. Coal taken to London by sea was called sea-coal to distinguish it from charcoal. Today it means coal washed up on the shore.

SEAM. A stratum of coal. The seams in the northern coalfield were given special names such as the *Beaumont seam,* the *Townley seam.* Transferred to general use we have the expression *a canny seam* meaning a good job.

SEEK. *Hadaway seek the milk* – go and bring the milk. *She's been oot seekin aal day* – She's been out all day asking for charity.

SEEK. Sick. *Seek ti deed* – Sick to death.

SEL. Self. Used in various combinations. *Hissel, mesel, worsels.*

SET-POT. Once found in every washhouse. It was a fixed pot with a fire underneath.

SETTING-STONE. A whetstone.

SHABBY. Applied to health when indifferent. *He's varry shabby thi' day.*

SHAFT. "A pit sunk from the surface; a vertical sinking, as distinguished from a *drift* or horizontal way into a mine. *Downcast shaft,* that by which air enters the mine. *Upcast shaft,* that by which it passes up, after traversing the workings of the colliery. *Shaft frame,* the elevated framework of wood or iron at bank. *Shaft framing,* the square framing at the top and bottom of the shaft into which the cage runs at the openings where the tubs are changed. *Shaft man,* a person employed to keep the shaft in repair. *Shaft pillars* or *shaft walls,* strong pillars of coal left round the bottom of a pit shaft. *Shaft rent,* rent formerly charged for the privilege of drawing up the shaft the coal worked from another royalty." Heslop.

SHAG. Covered with long hair. A *shag hat* was popular with keelmen and miners.

SHAKE-DOWN. A temporary bed made with a mattress and bedclothes on the floor.

SHAKES. Used only in the expression: *He's nee greet shakes, onyway* – He's not a reliable person.

SHAVER. A wag. *Whay a queer shaver he is.*

SHIELING. A shelter for sheep.

SHIFT. The time of working for one day where sets of men *(shifts)* relieve each other. In a colliery the first period of working is called the fore-*shift* and the next the back-*shift,* and the hewers themselves are similarly called the fore or back-*shift* according to their rotation in starting work. In factories, where continuous work is maintained, there is a day-*shift* and a night-*shift;* and at the end of the week a double-*shift* or a *shift* of twice the ordinary duration is sometimes worked, so as to turn the night men of one week into the day men of the next. A short-*shift* is a day's work of fewer than the ordinary number of hours.

SHIFT. To remove goods from one house to another. *Shiftin* – a removal.

SHIFTY. Unreliable.

SHIVE. A slice. *A shive of butter and breed.*

SHOOT. To shout. Gamekeeper: *Hullo, are you aware that there's no shooting here ?* Poacher: *Shootin, sor ? Aa's nivvor oppened me mooth.*

SHOOTIN. A common name for childbed.

SHORT. Shirt.

SHORT. Abrupt, ill-tempered. *He was quite short wi' me.*

SHOT. Rid of, clear off. *Get shot of* – get rid of a thing.

SHOUN. Shoes.

SHUGGYBOAT. A swing, once common at fairs, with seats across like a boat.

SHY. Unwilling, slow. *Yo'r varry shy wi' that baccy o' yors.*

SIC, SICCAN. Such. *Siccan a fight as we had I ne'er saw in a' my days.*

SIDE. Long, also steep.

"Aa'll tyek some o' this check say, a yard *side*. "In Newcastle, Percy Street was formerly known as *Side* Gate or *Sid*gate – that is, long street. The *Side* is still the name of the long and steep acclivity which connected the lower with the upper town of Newcastle. The evident meaning has led to its application in other places where similar steep bank-sides are characteristic. Gateshead (gate's heed, or head of the road) is thus, not infrequently, called Gate*side*; and Con*side* is a common form of Consett. *Side*, as denoting extent, is constantly used in the expression "the country-*side*," meaning either the adjacent district or the people living in a certain district. "The hyel country-*side* wis at the funeral." *Side* occurs in combination no less than eighty-five times in Northumberland place-names. Corsen*side*, Catcher*side*, Wood*side*, etc." Heslop.

SILLER. Silver.

SILLY. Young, innocent. A term of affection. *The bit bairn's asleep noo, silly thing.*

SINGIN HINNIE. The best known Geordie food. Peggy Howey (*The Geordie Cook Book*) tells us:

"The singing hinnie was so called as, when the butter and the cream melted during the baking, it sizzled on the hot girdle and was thought to be singing. An old tale is told of how this large tea-time scone first became known as a singing hinnie; a north country housewife was baking this scone for tea and on repeatedly being asked by her children if it was ready to eat, her final reply was 'No it's just singing, hinnies'."

SINKERS. Mining term for men who sink pit shafts.

SIT. The fit of a garment. *The coat sits him well.*

SKEDADDLE. To retreat quickly.

SKELP. To strike with the open hand particularly on the behind or the cheek. *Aa'll gie ye a skelp o' the lug.*

SKEP. A basket.

SKIN. To flog violently. Aa'll skin ye if aa get ahad on ye – If I catch you I will give you a good hiding.

SKINCH. A curious Northern word used in children's game to call a truce.

SKINT. Skinned or short of money. Compare *Skin-flint.*

SKITTERS. Diarrhoea.

SKYET-GOB. Fish-face.

SLACK. Small coal. Also means "insufficient in quantity." *Trade was nivvor se slack.*

SLAKE. A mud flat composed of *sleck* (ooze). The best known is *Jarrow Slake.*

SLEEKIT. Smooth skinned. *A sleekit cat.*

SLIP. A child's pinafore. *Pillow-slip* – a pillow case. Applied to a slim growing girl – *a bit slip iv a lass.*

SLIVER. A thin strip.

SLOP. Policeman.

SLORP. To make a noise when eating or drinking with a spoon. *He slorped his tea.*

SLUSH. Melting snow.

SMASH. An expletive to add emphasis.

SMIT. To infect.

SMITHEREENS. Small pieces. *It's gyen all ti smithereens.* It's broken in pieces.

SNAA. Snow.

SNACK. To snatch like a dog does.

SNAFFLE. To steal.

SNECK. The latch on a door or gate.

SNOB. A shoemaker. *Now run away amang the snobs an' stangies i' the Garth, man.* The Castle Garth at Newcastle was tenanted by shoemakers and tailors *(stangies).*

SNITCH. Nose. The nose, to tell tales. *Don't snitch on me.*

SNOOK. A beack-like projecting headland as *The Snook* at Holy Island.

SNOTTER. Mucus from the nose. *Snotter-cloot* means hand-kerchief.

SOD. A sot. *He's a greet sod.*

SO LONG. A parting salutation, meaning *goodbye for the present.* Said to derive from the Arabic *Salaam,* peace having been brought into England by soldiers who served abroad. I feel this explanation is far fetched.

SONNY. A friendly term for fellow.

SONSY. Good looking, pleasant. *Better by sonsy than soon up.* Newcastle proverb.

SPELK. A splinter of wood. *Aw've getten a spelk i' my hand.* Also a little slim person.

SPICE. Gingerbread. Also currants mixed with other food. *Spice-cake,* currant cake. *Spice-kail,* broth with currants mixed in.

SPITAL. Corruption of word *hospital.* Used in place names.

SPIT AN' IMAGE. Likeness. Applies either to a person or thing. *He's the spit an' image of his fethor.*

SPUGGY. House sparrow.

SPUNK. Courage, spirit. *He hes nee spunk at a'.* He has no guts.

SQUINT. A peep, not a defect of vision. *Let's hev a squint at the papers.*

STANNERS. Margins of rivers covered by deposits of stones and gravel.

STEEP. To soak, in washing clothes.

STINT. Fixed amount of work. An allowance of pasturage limited to grazing three sheep or one horse. Used in the expression – *he laboured without stint.*

STITCH. A sudden pain. *Aa've getten a stitch i' me side.*

STOB. A stump or post. Also a gibbet as in *Winter's Stob* near Elsdon.

STOOK. A pile of corn sheaves, twelve together, six on each side with two hood sheaves on the top.

STOOR. Dusty.

STOP. To stay, to dwell. *Where are ye stoppin?* – Where are you staying?. *Whe are ye stoppin wi?* – With whom are ye living?

STOPPLE. A tube. Usually used in *pipe stopple* – tobacco pipe.

STOT. To bounce. *The hailstones wis stotin off the hoose-tops.*

STOTTY CAKE. A large flat cake of bread – "oven bottom cake".

STOW. Stop. *Stow that, now!*

STRAA. Straw.

STRAIGHTS. Used only in the expression applied to a courting couple – *ganning straights* – meaning they are courting seriously.

STRAMP. To trample upon. *Dinna stramp ower the clean floor.*

STREET. A high road. The old pack-horse road between Newcastle and Carlisle was called the *Hee Street.* See also *Watling Street.*

STUMOR. Stupid. A person difficult to handle. *He's a stumor.*

STYFE. Choking smoke. A mining term.

SWANKY. Originally meant a strapping young fellow. Now means *posh.*

SWEIR. Unwilling, obstinate. *He's sweir ti pairt win his money –* He's unwilling to spend his money. *Hawkie is a sweir beast and Hawkie winna wade the watter*

SWIG. To take a heavy draught.

SYNE. Afterwards. *Simey Haa gat lam'd of a leg an' syne ran wallowin hame.*

T

TAB. A cigarette. A recent local word said to derive from a popular brand called *Ogden's Tabs.*

TACKLE. To accost. Also to do a job. *Aa'll tackle that job.*

TAGAREEN. Marine stores.

"A *tagareen man* had a floating shop which he towed about the tiers of ships, announcing his presence by a bell. His dealings were carried on by barter or cash, as may be convenient; and old rope, scrap-iron or other similar, unconsidered trifles, would be exchanged for the crockery or hardware with which the boat was stocked." Heslop.

Today a *tagareen man* is a scrap dealer.

TALLY. To keep account of goods.

"In delivering cargoes, one of the porter-pokemen usually "keeps *tally*." The number of bricks, or cheese, or bundles is counted as they are passed from hand to hand, the last man but one repeating the figures aloud. If the articles are counted singly they are called out up to the nineteenth; but instead of calling out "twenty" the word *tally* is substituted; thus – "eighteen, nineteen, *tally*." The score is then marked by a simple line drawn with a piece of chalk. After four strokes are made, the fifth is drawn through them diagonally from left to right, like the cross-bar of a field gate, and the symbol one hundred is thus indicated. In counting articles that can be lifted in groups the tale is thus made – "five, ten, fifteen, *tally*." Heslop.

TALLY-MAN. A credit draper.

TAPPY-LAPPY. To rush aimlessly and blindly. *The twee boxers went ti'd tappy-lappy like a lowse winda shutter flappin i' the wind.*

TASH. Moustache.

TATIE. A potato. *Tatie-boggle* – a scarecrow.

TATTY. Matted. *What a tatty heed Mary hes.*

TAWSE. A leather strap with end split into five *toes* or fingers used for hitting children.

TEASER. A problem, an annoyance. *That's a teaser for ye*

TEE. Usually in the expression *It fits him tiv a tee* – It fits him perfectly. Origin uncertain.

TEEM. To pour. *Teem oot the tea* – pour out the tea. Also a pit term for *teeming* coals out of the waggons into the ship. The man in charge was called a *teemer.* Used to express weather, *It's teeming cats and dogs.*

TELLY-PIE. A tell-tale. From *telly* – talkative, and *pie* – a magpie There is the famous children's rhyme, *Tellypie tit, yor tongue shall be slit, an aall the bairns i' wor street shall hev a little bit.*

TEN O'CLOCK. A snack taken at that time. *He' ye had yor ten o'clock yit?*

TEW. A hard and laboured effort. Used with slightly different meaning in several expressions. *Aa've tew'd at the job till aa's paid* – I've struggled at the job but I'm now beaten.

THINK-SHYEM. To feel ashamed.

THRUM. To purr. *The cat's happy; d'ye hear hor thrummin?* Also means to make a drumming noise. *The Thrum* at Rothbury was the place where the Coquet narrowed and formed a cascade.

THUMPIN. Big, hearty. *Here's thumpin luck to yon toon, let's have a hearty drink upon't.*

TICE. Entice.

TIG. A sharp blow as in the game of *tiggy.*

TIME. Apprenticeship. *Aa served me time tiv a shoemaker.*

TIMMER. Timber. *Cross timmers* – the cross beams of a building. Food is called *belly-timmer.*

TOMMY NODDY. The puffin. Also applies to dwarfs. *Tommynoddy; big head an' little body.* A taunt.

TO REETS. Right. Usually in the expression *put to reets* – to keep orderly.

TORMIT. A turnip.

TRANSLATOR. A Castle Garth cobbler. Worn boots and shoes were bought and cobbled, or *translated*, into wearable articles by those now nearly obsolete craftsmen, whose shops lined the Castle Garth Stairs in Newcastle, and divided the Black Gate shops with those of the old clothiers.

"But man, when the Garth aw espied,
Aw was nowther to had or to bin, man;
For *translators* and tailors aw cried,
But the devel a yane aw could find, man."
Song, *The High Level Bridge.*

TOWSHER. Scruffy person.

TRASH. To wear out with overwork. *Aa's trashed ti deed* – I'm worn to death.

TRET. Treated. *The bairns had been badly tretten.*

TRIM. To level coals as they are loaded on to a ship. *"A set of men called trimmers, who with shovels and rakes distribute the coal or trim the cargo."* Greenwell, *Coal Trade Terms,* 1888.

TUB. "Originally a mining bucket, now specially applied to the open-topped box of wood or iron, mounted on wheels, in which coal is brought from the face to the surface. It has supplanted the old "corf," which was a basket carried on a tram. The tram and *tub* are now, in most cases, a single structure. The *tub*, containing twenty-four pecks, has an inside measurement of three feet in length, thirty inches in width, and twenty-six in depth. *Tub-loaders*, hewers who hew and fill the empty tubs at times when the pit is not drawing coals." Heslop.

TWANK. To punish with a strap or cane.

TYEK. To take. One of those common Northumbrian words with many grades of meaning. *He tyeks efter the fethor* – He is like his father. *Bella an' hims tyen on* – Bella and him have become attached.

46

U

UNBEKNAAN. Without knowledge of.

UNCANNY. Supernatural. *She hes an uncanny way wiv her.*

UNCO. Very, He was *unco glad.*

UNDERSTRAPPER. Underling.

UNTHANK. A place name found three times in Northumberland. Probably meant the land was difficult to work or *ungrateful.*

UPCAST. To bring up as an example. *Yor elwis upcastin yor greet cosin Jim, just as if thor wis nebody ekwil te him.*

UPSTANNIN. Standing. A mining term applied to old workings where the roof had not fallen in. An *Upstanning wage* was a regular wage paid even when no work was or could be done.

UPTAK. Understanding. *He wes slow i' the uptak.*

US. Used for me. *Wiv us* – with me.

V

VAR NIGH. Very near.

VAST. A great deal. *Thor wis a vast o' folk i' the chepil.*

VENNEL. A narrow lane, also a drain.

VIEWER. The manager of a colliery.

VINE. A lead pencil.

W

WAFTERS. Swords made with blunt edges for performers, like the sword dancers. They also had handles at each end.

WAG. Truant. *Play the wag* – to play truant from school.

WAG AT THE WAA. A caseless clock in which the weights and the *wagging* pendulum are visible.

WARK. Work. Not a local word but a local pronunciation. The famous doctor joke depends on this pronunciation. The doctor asked Geordie "Can you walk"? *Wark?* Geordie replied, *I canna even waalk,* meaning "Work ? I can't even walk."

WAT CHEOR. A common Geordie salutation meaning *What cheer.*

WEE, WEENY. Little, small. *Move up a wee bit. A weeny bit of cheese.*

WELT. To lash.

WHEY AYE. Of course.

WHINGE. To whine, applied to dogs and children. *A whingin bairn.*

WHISHT. Be quiet. *Whisht lads, haad yor gobs* (Lambton Worm).

WID. With it.

WIFE. Any staid woman, married or single *Hi canny wife! Aad wives' tales. Midwife. Fishwife.*

WIG. A tea-cake, a yeasted cake with kneading in it. "A spice *wig*" is one with currants. *Tea-cake* is the modern name for this. The story goes that a Newcastle lass, in service in London, enquired where she could get some *wigs*. Being directed to a barber's shop, she astonished the "artiste" by asking the price of his "spice *wigs*," as she wanted half a dozen for tea." Heslop.

WIN. Used specially in coal mining to describe arriving by sinking at the coal seam *to win the coal.*

WIV. With. *Wiv a coal in each hand.*

WIVOOT. Without. *It's lone wivoot him, that bonny lad o' mine.*

WORM. A serpent. The name given to the legendary monsters described in so many ballads. The *Lambton Worm* is the best known. But there was the *Laidley Worm* of Spindleston Heugh near Bamburgh, and the "Dragon-Worm" of Sockburn in Durham.

WORRIT. To worry. *He set his dog on to worrit wor cat.*

WRANG. Wrong. *Wrang iv his heed* – dearranged.

Y

YAP. A brat, an impudent lad.

YAKKER. A *pit yakker* is the northern term for a pitman. Possibly derived from the word *yark* meaning "a heavy blow."

YALLA CLAY. A hearthstone. Now remembered because *Cushie Butterfield* sold them.

YAMMER. To whine or complain. *Giv ower yammerin* – Stop whining. Especially applied to children.

YARK. To thrash soundly. *Aa'll yark yor hide for ye.*

YEL. Ale. **YELHOOSE.** – alehouse.

YUL-DOO, YULE-BABBY. "A baby figure made of a flat cake of gingerbread or currant cake, and sold to children. The arms are folded across, and two currants are put in for eyes. *Yul-doos* are probably so-called because made from the *yule* or Christmas dough. *Yule-cakes*, so-called elsewhere, are not known in Northumberland."